Sandy Creek
NEW YORK

An Imprint of Sterling Publishing
387 Park Avenue South
New York, NY 10016

Text © 2014 by The Salariya Book Company Ltd
Illustrations © 2014 by The Salariya Book Company Ltd

ISBN 978-1-4351-5629-6

Author: Jacqueline Morley
Editors: Karen Barker Smith, Caroline Coleman
Illustrations: Pam Hewetson, Nick Hewetson, David Antram,
Gerald Wood

Manufactured in Heyuan, Guangdong Province, China
Lot #:
2 4 6 8 10 9 7 5 3 1
07/14

Contents

FASHION

The History

of Clothes

Jacqueline Morley

Sandy Creek
NEW YORK

The Ancient World

Fashion has been around for a long time. Archaeologists have found the remains of animal-skin garments from 23,000 years ago decorated with shells and beads. This suggests that the urge to make clothes for other reasons than just keeping warm is basic to human nature. The first sewn garments were made of stitched skins, and later, of woven cloth. The earliest fashions that are known with any certainty are those of Mesopotamia and ancient Egypt, about 3000 BC. The rulers of these civilizations wore the finest cloth and jewelry to reflect their power.

Paleolithic (Old Stone Age) family, c. 21,000 BC, wearing skins decorated with seashells, ivory beads, and animal teeth.

Early Mesopotamian priest and queen (above). His tufted skirt copies earlier garments made of skins. The queen wears a magnificent gold wreath.

Crook and flail (royal emblems)

False beard

Royal headdresses

Wig of human hair

Jeweled and enameled collar

Transparent overtunic

Narrow sheath

Gold armband

This Egyptian pharaoh and his queen, about 1300 BC, wear headdresses and jewelry that proclaim them to be gods on Earth, for that is what the Egyptians believed their kings to be.

Long pleated loincloth

Toe-strap sandals

Fact: Egyptians
• White linen was in fashion for 3,000 years. Men wore it as loincloths, and women as narrow sheath dresses. Rich people added an overtunic of expensive transparent linen.
• Men and women wore wigs, perfume, and heavy eye makeup.
• Workers often went naked.

Woolen headband

Tunic (chiton)

Large cloak (himation)

Thonged sandals

Ancient Greek gold necklace and ring. A Greek goldsmith's work was delicate, while the Romans preferred chunky jewelry.

The ancient Greeks wore tunics made of rectangles of draped cloth, fastened with a brooch on the shoulders, and often open at the side. For warmth they added a cloak made of another large rectangle of cloth. Men might wear the cloak alone, without a tunic, leaving a shoulder bare. The earliest Greek clothes were woolen. The use of thin linen (a 6th-century BC fashion influence from Asia Minor) brought wide, gathered tunics into favor. Roman dress was similar, though the typical male garment, a cloak known as a toga, was semicircular.

Fact: Greeks
• Rich Greeks wore brilliant colors but the poor were not supposed to wear dyed cloth. An Athenian decree forbade them from going to the theater in clothes dyed reddish-brown.

Right, a typical Roman family. Roman women (and Greek ones also) covered their heads with their cloak when outdoors.

Fact: Romans
• Wearing a toga was a sign of Roman citizenship. Slaves were not allowed to wear one.
• Togas were draped in increasingly complicated ways and got larger as time went by. By the 1st century AD they could be over 6 meters across and very cumbersome.
• In Imperial times (from 27 BC) rich Romans wore costly silks imported from China.

Ancient Greek couple (above). The woman has doubled her tunic over at the top before pinning and belting it. Its hem is embroidered.

Short tunic

Toga

Beneath their tunics, Greek and Roman people probably wore garments like these (above). These images were found in a Roman floor mosaic.

Tunic girdled at hips and waist

Cloak (palla)

The Dark Ages

When 5th-century barbarian invaders conquered Rome, its traditions of luxurious living survived at Byzantium (modern Istanbul). Byzantium was the capital of the surviving eastern half of Rome's former empire and controlled the trade from China, Persia, and India in silks, spices, and gems, making it immensely rich. Its emperor and courtiers lived in the greatest magnificence.

The man and woman below (right) are in the type of clothes worn, with little variation, by the Anglo-Saxons (in England) and the Franks (in France) from the 7th to the 11th centuries. Both wear tunics (the woman's is called a gown) over narrow-wristed undertunics. The woman's cloak is a circle of fabric put on over the head. She wears a kerchief—a cloth covering her head—as women did in public. Nobles' clothes were made of better cloth with more ornament.

Tablion, a decorative panel denoting rank

Jeweled diadem

Ropes of pearls

Jeweled collar

Kerchief

Semicircular cloak

Circular cloak

Silk tunic

Silk cloak

Shoes with ankle decorations

Undertunic

Overgown

Embroidery of gold thread, set with emeralds

Above left, a 6th-century Byzantine emperor and empress in gold-embroidered silk tunics and large semicircular cloaks, which replaced togas.

Fact: Byzantium

• Until the 6th century, silk had to be imported from China, for only the Chinese knew how to make it. Then (according to legend), two missionary monks sent by the Byzantine empress smuggled silkworms out of China hidden in a hollow cane. Byzantium was then able to start its own silk production.

• Precious stones, pearls, and shimmering gold thread were used as decorations.

• The richest weaves and most expensive dyes were reserved for the emperor's family.

7th-century Frankish brooch (left) and buckle (far left) of "cloisonné", made by filling compartments with colored enamel. The method came from the near east, via Byzantium.

Meanwhile, in war-torn Europe merchants feared traveling, so luxuries were scarce. Most people wore homespun wool and never thought of fashion. Yet some notion of Byzantine styles trickled through and, as conditions improved, rulers tried to copy them. The 9th-century Frankish ruler Charlemagne was buried in his ceremonial robes—tunics of the richest Byzantine silk, one set with rubies. For everyday wear, he preferred traditional northern dress—a knee-length tunic and braies (long breeches, bound at the lower leg).

Viking bead necklace, hung with trinkets

Cloak brooch

Dress brooch

Animal-skin cloak

10th-century Vikings in their version of the north European tunic, cloak, and braies (below left).

Open gown

Loose braies

Deep decorative border

Gown

Below: Viking ribbon for garment edging. It could be woven in complicated patterns.

One Viking wears his braies loose (middle). His wife has a sideless top-gown held by brooches.

Fact: Vikings
• Rich Vikings wore large gold collars and brooches to show off their wealth.
• Warlords rewarded their followers after battle by giving them heavy gold neck rings and arm bands.
• Vikings were enterprising merchants, going on long and dangerous journeys to foreign markets in search of goods to sell. They even brought back Byzantine silks for the few Vikings who could afford them.

Viking women hung toiletry implements (ear and nail cleaners) from a brooch at their chest.

Medieval Times

Variations on the tunic, overtunic, and cloak continued to be worn throughout Europe in the 11th, 12th, and 13th centuries. Nobles wore fine versions and peasants had hard-wearing ones. Tunics, even men's, trailed around the feet and had side or back lacing that shaped them to the chest. Sleeves were enormously wide at the wrist.

The simpler 13th century styles, widening to the hem, often had sleeveless overtunics. In the 14th century, men's tunics were much shorter and more body-hugging. By 1350, they barely covered the hips and were worn with a low belt.

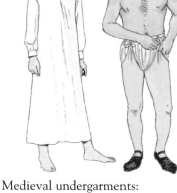

Medieval undergarments: Men's hose were in separate legs and were only attached at the top. Women wore a simple undergown.

Fact: Medieval
• Knights returning from the Crusades brought back a taste for luxury—rich weaves, silks, and furs.
• By the end of the 14th century, the points on men's shoes were so long that they had to be fastened to their knees by chains.

A 12th-century queen and nobleman. Both wear a wide-sleeved overtunic or overgown. The queen's is mostly hidden by her cloak.

Kerchief

Undergown

Overtunic

Sleeves of overgown

Plaits with false hair added

1150: Side lacing and cuffs so long they have to be knotted.
1170: Three-quarter-length fur overtunic.

1240: The children wear typical 13th-century gowns—narrow-wristed, flaring, and often unbelted.

1250: A new type of top garment with slits for the arms. It was fashionable to let its sleeves hang empty.

1280: Married women still covered their heads and sometimes wore a wimple—a cloth from neck to chin.

1317: The man's hooded and dagged overgown is open from shoulder to hem; the woman's has deep, cut-away armholes.

A wealthy man and his wife, about 1240. He wears a full cloak, narrow-wristed, calf-length tunic and undertunic.

Her flat cap, hairnet, and linen chin band are typical of the time. So is the cord holding her cloak.

The couple below are from about 1380. The woman's scooped neck and figure-hugging, tightly-buttoned overgown are typically 14th-century. The cuffs of the overgown sleeves end in long streamers of cloth, known as tippets.

The man is wearing a houppelande, a garment that replaced the cloak. It was often ankle-length.

Linen band (barbette)

Fur cap

Linen coif (underbonnet)

Fur collar

Face-framing plaits

Undergown sleeves

Tippet

Buttoned sleeves

Brooch closing undergown

Hanging purse

Slit for access to hanging purse beneath

Long-pointed shoes

"Dagged" (slit) edges

Front slit for ease of riding a horse

1330: Noblewoman with a long ceremonial train and a wimple. The sides of her overgown are laced.

1359: Nobleman in the new, short tunic. His wife's overgown is cut away so that the front is just a strip.

1365: Fashionable man in a short cape; girl in a striped overgown with elbow-length sleeves and tippets.

1380: Man in a cape and patterned houppelande. The cuffs of his undergown cover his hands.

1395: Women wore houppelandes too. This has immensely wide sleeves, and her headdress is dagged to match.

15th Century

Burgundian enameled hat brooch with a cameo portrait. Men wore large brooches on their hats and women wore them in their hair.

Fact: Late Medieval styles

• Some men wore parti-colored garments and hose (the left side different from the right).
• Footwear went to new lengths, with points stiffened with whalebone and pattens (separate wooden soles).
• Sleeves came in all shapes, from empty, trailing ones to those with stuffed shoulders or sleeves made of small pieces joined up with lacing.

By the 15th century, fashion was not just for kings, queens, and the nobility. Trade increased throughout the Middle Ages, and by now some merchant families were so rich that they lent money to kings. Such wealthy people could afford the best furs and richest silks, and those who were a little less rich did their best to copy them. The authorities often passed laws to try to stop them from doing so—if everyone who could afford it was allowed to wear fine things, how could people identify the real nobles? As well as nobles in castles and peasants working the land, there were now many comfortable, well-off people living in towns, who liked to show their prosperity by being seen in expensive clothes. Styles changed faster as people competed with each other, and trends were taken to extremes. Women's headgear grew fantastically wide or tall, and young men wore extremely short garments with padded shoulders and sleeves. Regional differences became more pronounced. It was easy to tell an Italian from a Burgundian, for example, from the way they dressed. The rich Duke of Burgundy set the fashions for northern Europe.

1416 French courtiers: The man's houppelande has fur-lined sleeves, patterned with crowns.

The woman's arms emerge from slits in her trailing sleeves that hang empty.

1430 Italians: The man has bag sleeves, tight at the wrists, while the woman's hair is dressed over a frame.

1448: Men's gowns are shorter and tightly belted to form neat folds. Pattens support the long-toed hose.

1450: The height of Burgundian fashion! A "steeple" headdress with a veil held out over a wire frame.

Mid 15th-century couple (below). The woman is wearing a high-waisted, broad-belted gown.

Her hair, dressed in a net on each side of her head, is topped with a padded roll.

The folds of the man's short overgown are padded and stitched to keep their shape.

The flap of cloth that hides the gap between the separate legs is called a codpiece.

V-necked gown

Heart-shaped headdress

Hat with trailing end wound around the neck

To stop the braies from showing under the very short top garments, the legs of the hose were tied to the bottom of the doublet with a codpiece in-between. Sleeves were separate and tied as well.

Fur collar

Padded chest

Fact: Renaissance

By the close of the 15th century, medieval ways of dressing had mostly vanished.
• Floating veils, pointed shoes, big headdresses, and long trains disappeared.
• Men's long gowns were quite out of fashion, except for old or pompous people.
• Instead of falling in folds, men's clothes were boxy with square shoulders.

Padded sleeves

1495

1495: Three young Venetians. Italian women did not wear the elaborate headgear of northern Europe. All three wear the new fashion for showing the shirt or chemise through gaps between the sleeve pieces. The man on the right wears an extremely short doublet and no overgown. Older people thought this was shocking.

Undergown

11

16th Century

The flowing tunics of medieval times were now a thing of the past. The 16th-century fashion demanded a stiff, almost sculpted look, and the clothes could almost stand up by themselves. This was partly due to the richly patterned brocades and heavy velvets that were used, and partly because garments were stiffened and padded in ways that had nothing to do with the human shape. Bombast (a stuffing of horsehair and rags) produced men's shoulders of enormous width; later in the century, it gave them pumpkin-shaped thighs and padded bellies tapering to a point. Women's chests and stomachs were completely flattened by rigid corsets reinforced with strips of metal or whalebone.

Merman pendant. His body is made of a huge pearl.

1514: German couple (right). The man's garments are "slashed" (slit to show the cloth below). This was a fashion fad that lasted, in less extreme forms, throughout the century.

Legwear was now formed of upper and lower hose. This man's upper hose cover the knees, but during the century they got shorter and wider and were often stuffed. In this form, they were called trunk hose.

Gold chains

Slashed doublet

Slashed overgown

Upper hose

Lower hose

Fact: Footwear
• The blunt-toed shoes of the first half of this century were padded to seem as broad as they were long.
• Hose were now made of knitted wool instead of cloth, which was a much better fit.

Plumed cap

Bodice collar

Sleeve in several pieces

The woman wears a gown of heavy silk, boldly patterned in bands. Its bodice opening is laced across. Later in the century, this area was filled by a stomacher—a rigid, fabric-covered triangle. The man's shirt forms a decorative frill at his neck. During the century, this grew larger and stiffer and developed into the ruff.

Long girdle

Blunt-toed shoes

12

King Henry
VIII,
1536

Flat cap

Wide fur collar

Slashed doublet

Codpiece

Fur-lined
overgown

Jerkin
with deep
U-neck

The 1530s
cube look:
the flat cap,
padded doublet,
and wide-collared
overgown with
bulging sleeves form
a totally square figure.

Above, the Spanish
farthingale and, below,
the French farthingale,
a variation that appeared
in the late 1570s.

Fact: Farthingales

• Spain, the richest country in Europe at this time, was the source of many fashions: the stiff ruff around the neck, the vogue for black, and the farthingale—a series of rigid hoops supporting skirts.

• The farthingale appeared in the late 15th century. It spread to Italy, where it was thought indecent and was banned. By 1500 it had reached France, and by 1550 all the fashionable women of Europe were wearing it.

Queen Elizabeth I, 1592

Ruff
supported
by wire
frame

Ruff of
starched
lace

Stomacher

Jewel-encrusted
brocade over
French
farthingale

1546
1550
1555
1560
1571
1581
1588
1595

1546: Skirted doublet and overgown.
1550: Farthingale under open skirt and cushion-sleeved overgown.

1555: Short Spanish cloak.
1560: Softer Italian woman's gown and men's short jerkin, doublet, and hose.

1571: High Spanish ruff encircling neck, open sleeve caught at wrist, skirt closed with ribbon ties.

1581: Open ruff and French farthingale; cape and brief trunk hose with canions (upper leg coverings).

1588: Wide ruff, belly-padded doublet.
1595: Stuffed trunk hose; boy in soft collar and breeches.

17th Century

1630: High-waisted, long-skirted doublet, cloak, and breeches in slashed and braided satin. The plumed hat, riding boots, and lavish use of lace are typical of the time.

Wide-brimmed hat

Long curls

Deep lace collar

Lace cuffs

Wide-topped boots with lace-trimmed linings

Early in the 17th century, the stiff Spanish style gave way to a softer look. Ruffs became drooping collars and stiff brocades were replaced by lightweight silks and lace. Women's gowns were wide-shouldered and full-sleeved with gathered skirts of billowing silk. After 1670 the female silhouette was narrower and stiffer. Men added lavish flounces of lace at the neck, wrists, and knees. In the 1660s, they were wearing "petticoat" breeches with trims of looped ribbon and legs so wide they looked like a skirt. This was too outrageous to last long. In the 1670s, a new garment, the vest, a simple, narrow-sleeved, front-buttoning jacket, appeared. With narrow breeches and a coat, it formed the earliest three-piece suit.

Lace-trimmed collar

1636: The sloping shape of the collar is continued by the swelling sleeves. The bodice is seamed to fit snugly. It was fashionable to show some underskirt.

1618: Stiff open ruff, short-skirted doublet, baggy breeches, and shoes with large rosettes.

1634: The man's hair is longer, his breeches tighter, and his collar and boots are draped in lace.

1640: Loose-ended breeches, decorated at the hem, meet boots with "bucket" tops.

1645: Side ringlets, high waist, almost off-the-shoulder neckline, and skirt drawn up to show underskirt.

1646: Short doublet showing shirt bloused out over ribbon-trimmed breeches, boot tops filled with lace.

Court lady of 1690

Necklines are no longer wide and slipping off the shoulders. Instead, the fashionable look is narrow-shouldered, with the chest squashed up toward the chin with firm corseting.

Narrow, three-quarter sleeves

Muff

Falls of lace

Fontange

Beauty patch

Tiered underskirt

Overskirt

Above, a pendant of ivory, enamel and gold, in the form of a "momento mori" (a reminder of death). Repeated plagues and wars meant death was frequently encountered. Skulls and coffins were common motifs in jewelry.

Fact: 17th century
• High heels began to be worn and by the end of the century they were frequently over 3 inches high.
• Long hair was fashionable. Both sexes favored wearing wigs rather than caring for all that hair.

The headdress of wired lace, attached to a linen cap, was called a fontange. It was typical of the 1690s.

"Patches"—small dots of black velvet or silk stuck to the face—were thought to be attractive.

The deeply frilled velvet overskirt matches the bodice. The skirt is looped back to show its decorative lining and arranged to form a bustle and short train.

The skirt and underskirt are still made separately from the bodice. Underskirts are no longer meant to be hidden. They are made from expensive materials and have become an important part of the gown. This one is made in three deep flounces.

1660: Petticoat breeches.
1663: Longer hair, more ribbon, and flounces at the knee.

1674: Necklines are higher and narrower, trimmings more elaborate, and ornamental aprons are in fashion.

1678: Return to simpler fashion—a long-sleeved, fitted coat worn with a wide-brimmed hat for men.

1683: Buttoned coat and winter greatcoat. The brim of the hat is "cocked" (bent up).

1693: Women's hunting clothes in male style. A couple in walking clothes—both carry muffs.

18th Century

A wealthy Englishwoman of 1715 in riding clothes. Her cocked hat, cravat, and full-skirted coat with wide buttoned-back cuffs copy the latest fashions for men.

Cocked hat

Man's cravat

Pockets buttoned to match cuffs

Women now took the fashion lead. Coats and breeches remained the rule for men, the coat becoming slimmer as the century progressed. Meanwhile, women varied their shape amazingly. At first, skirts swelled out over underskirts reinforced with hoops. The width then moved to the sides, supported by "panniers" (the French word for baskets), which were cane constructions worn over the hips. In the 1770s, women pulled their hair up over tall pads or wire frames and topped them with fantastic decorations. By the 1780s broad hats exaggerated the width of women's heads, and the most fashionable women wore a plain white dress like a chemise (a sleeved petticoat), sashed at the waist.

Fact: 18th century
• By the 1740s, fashionable skirts were so wide (up to 4 meters across) that women had to turn sideways to get through doors.
• Men of the upper classes, who used to carry swords, now carried canes instead. But the custom of buttoning the coat from left to right (originally to let the right hand slip in easily to draw the sword) was by now standard practice. It is the same today.

Diamond brooch in the form of a bow, for the top of a stomacher.

1707: Frills are in fashion; frilled muslin cap and deep, stiff flounces on the skirt and underskirt.

1726: The coat of the early part of the century, nipped at the waist, with deep cuffs and a stiffened skirt.

1731: "Sack" gown of embroidered silk, falling in a train of loose pleats from the shoulders.

1744: A humbler style; the customary low neckline is filled in by a fichu—a square of fine white linen.

1749: Panniers at their widest; a lace cap is always worn, except on the grandest occasions.

Because of her skirt, the mother rides side-saddle (breeches were unthinkable for women). Her jacket folds back to form revers.

Revers

Plain skirt

The father (below) wears a country frock coat. These had a turned-down collar and narrow cuffs or none at all; their cut-away front was more convenient for riding.

Round country hat
Short waistcoat
No cuffs

Pants *Riding boots* *Chemise dress*

1770s underwear (above): chemise, long corset, and small panniers.

1770s English family in the country (right). The parents wear clothes designed for riding. English aristocrats enjoyed the country and spent so much time there that it became smart for young men to be seen in country clothes, even in London. The fashion caught on abroad—by the 1780s, elegant Frenchmen (no lovers of the countryside) were copying the English country style.

1790s drawers (above) with separate legs joined only to the waistband.

The little boy and his sister are wearing children's styles. Comfortable clothes for children were a new idea. Until this period they were dressed in smaller versions of adult fashions, including ruffs, corsets, and sometimes even wigs.

1759 1770 1771 1777 1781 1786

1759: Narrower coat with a turn-down collar; full skirts but no exaggerated panniers for day wear.

1770: Court evening dress. Big panniers are no longer worn by day but formal styles are slow to change.

1771: Cut-away coat front showing the now shorter waistcoat. 1777: "Polonaise" gown, gathered at the back.

1781: English smart casual wear for town—a plain wool riding coat, round-brimmed country hat, and boots.

1786: A French redingote (from "riding coat") and muslin chemise gown, displaying the new simplicity.

Early 19th Century

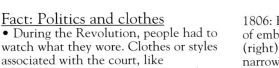

At the end of the 18th century, when freedom and equality were in the air, fashions became simpler and less constricting. These ideals were taken to extremes during the French Revolution. While the revolution lasted, elegant French people dressed like workers and peasants. When order was restored, fashionable clothing returned. However, people soon forgot that the wearing of pants had started out as a symbol of revolution—by 1820, they were standard wear for men.

1794: Clothes of the Revolution. Working class pants, apron, and a specially designed "citizen's costume" that did not catch on.

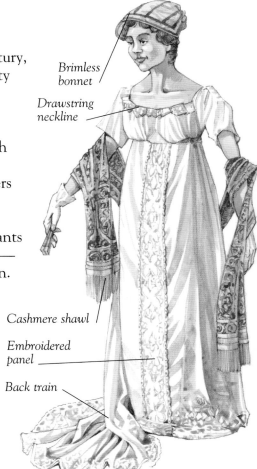

Brimless bonnet

Drawstring neckline

Cashmere shawl

Embroidered panel

Back train

Fact: Politics and clothes

• During the Revolution, people had to watch what they wore. Clothes or styles associated with the court, like panniers and powdered hair, aroused suspicions. The wearer could easily be condemned as a traitor and executed.

• Keen revolutionaries tried to show that they were men of the people by wearing pants. Until then, these had only been worn by workers and children— gentlemen had worn breeches.

1806: Evening dress of embroidered muslin (right). High-waisted, narrow-skirted garments had been in fashion since the end of the last century. White was the favored color and a long cashmere shawl was the favorite accessory.

1798: French chemise with ribbon decoration based on the way aristocrats were tied for execution.

1802: Skimpy dresses, sometimes dampened to cling, were supposed to give the look of a Greek statue.

1808: Men now wore top hats and long, tight breeches or nearly skin-tight pants known as pantaloons.

1811: Evening dress, still high-waisted, but much more vivid in color and decoration than before.

1814: Lady's traveling coat worn with a small fur cape.
1815: Two young girls in walking clothes.

Top hat
(essential wear)

Silk
cravat

Wide-brimmed
bonnet

Wide collar
and revers

Broad lace collar

Gilt
buttons

Long tight cuffs

Pleated
bodice

Gathered
trouser
front

1828 men's underwear (above): muslin shirt with a tucked front and a high, stiffened collar with points.

1828: The man is wearing a formal "tail" coat, a descendant of the country riding coat. As often happened, the sports clothes of one period became formal wear in the next. (A version of this outfit is still seen today at fancy weddings.)

1830 women's underwear (above): a tight-waisted, back-laced corset over a chemise with padded sleeves.

1828 walking dress of printed cotton. The look is still high-waisted but the skirt is fuller (held out by layers of petticoats). Bonnet, collar, and padded sleeves emphasize the top half of the body, while flounces at the hem echo this.

1817   1823   1828   1829   1829   1830

1817: A walking dress, its wider hem embellished with padded bands.
1823: Hats are wider, waists lower.

1828: Double-breasted day coat with "leg-of-mutton" sleeves, full at the shoulder and tight at the wrist.

1829: Emphatic hats and hem decorations were in fashion. A wide neckline sets off the tiny waist.

1829: Single-breasted greatcoat with padded sleeves; for evening wear, a tailcoat and pantaloons.

1830: Wide shoulders taken to extremes, with balloon sleeves, flounces, and a lower waistline.

Late 19th Century

Below, an 1840s gold bracelet in the shape of a snake. Its enameled head is set with diamonds.

Fact: Hems and crinolines

• By the 1850s skirts could measure 10 meters around the hem, sometimes more if made of very thin silk or muslin.
• In 1856, a Frenchman patented the crinoline, a frame of flexible steel hoops that replaced all the petticoats that had previously been needed under these skirts.

1840s underwear:
1) Chemise and drawers; 2) then a tight-waisted corset and a camisole; 3) next, a petticoat of stiff woven horsehair;
4) then one reinforced with stitching; 5) over this, two or more starched layers;
6) finally, a muslin one with a fancy hem.

Trade boomed in the 19th century, creating a rich middle class that displayed its wealth by wearing expensive clothes. Men were expected to dress seriously for the serious job of making money, but their wives and daughters could be as gaudy as they liked. Fashion magazines started to appear, and from the 1850s on, women's fashions were incredibly extravagant in fabrics and trimmings. Poorly-paid working women spent long hours hand-sewing huge crinoline skirts and, later, bustles. The invention of the sewing machine did little to help them; it only increased the demand for trimmings. Critics who said corsets were unhealthy and bustles ridiculous went unheeded. Only the concept of sportswear, first appearing in the 1870s, made simpler styles acceptable.

Necklaces in the form of snakes were popular too. The snake went around the throat in the form of a chain and often had a heart-shaped locket hanging from its jaws.

1833   1834   1836   1837   1840   1845   1847

1833: Winter outdoor gown of velvet with embroidered panels, worn with a muff, bonnet, and veil.

1834: Men's day wear, tight-waisted, with sloping shoulders.
1836: Women's sleeves have gone droopy.

1837: Big sleeves are out, little bonnets are in. Mother and daughter both have skirts with lots of trimming.

1840: A new waistline, V-shaped in front.
1845: Huge shawls over wide skirts made women look triangular.

1847: Man in a high-buttoned waistcoat and shirt with standing collar. Woman with winter fur muff.

1866: Walking dress of striped silk, worn over a crinoline. The first crinolines were circular, producing a "tea-cozy" skirt, but the rounded front was inconvenient and made it difficult to get near other people without tilting the frame up at the back. 1860s crinolines were much flatter in front but were elongated behind, forming a train.

The tiny brimless bonnet is tied with an enormous bow beneath the chin.

Glass buttons

Slightly raised waist

The front-buttoning bodice was separate from the skirt. Some skirts had two tops, one for day and one for evening wear.

Oversleeve

Narrow undersleeve

This dress has quite a small train by the standards of the 1860s. Some crinolines stuck out far behind their wearers.

Fringed braid trim

The crinoline frame (below), made of flexible steel hoops, held the petticoat and skirt well clear of the legs. The man wears a vest with open armpits.

Lace shawl

1871: Skirts are held up in the small of the back by a horsehair or wire bustle. The man wears a loose jacket.

1875: Fur-lined coat with big collar and cuffs. The woman's dress has an open overskirt bunched up over a bustle.

1877: Evening dress, showing how much skirts have slimmed in ten years, with all the fullness at the back.

1880: Very tight skirts are briefly in fashion, but bustles were to make a comeback in the mid-1890s.

1880: Clothes designed for sport; cap, jacket, and knickerbockers for shooting; bathing dress; cycling gear.

1900–1929

Before the First World War, fashionable clothes were elaborate and needed a lot of care and attention to be worn properly. However, women gained more independence and freedom during the war, and afterwards they wanted that to continue. Designers responded with shorter-skirted styles, very daring at the time. Less wealthy people could now buy fashionable styles too, thanks to the mass manufacturing of machine-made clothes.

Lace-trimmed hat

Straw boater

"Choker" neckline

Double-breasted jacket

Stiff shirt collar

Fact: Prewar
• Rich women had several changes of clothes per day: informal day wear, morning walking dresses, tea gowns for receiving friends, afternoon dresses for visiting, dinner gowns, and full evening dresses.

1910 underwear: Suspenders, attached to the bottom of the corset, have replaced garters for holding up women's stockings.

Long gloves

1905 woolen traveling dress

1904 flannel boating suit

1901

1905

1908

1910

1912

1913

1914

1918

1901: The turn of the century shape, made by the "S-bend" corset, pinched in at the back.

1905: Motoring coat, worn with a flat cap.
1908: Waistless dress by rebel French designer, Paul Poiret.

1910: Poiret's slender look has caught on, worn with very wide hats, and here, with a long fur stole.

1912: A bridesmaid's dress with low V-neck.
1913: Wrap-over skirts allow for walking in ankle-tight styles.

1914: Overtunics are popular on dresses and as part of suits.
1918: A raincoat with raglan sleeves.

1925: Short silk evening dress, decorated with heavy embroidery of glass beads and imitation pearls. The embroidery design and the hanging girdle were inspired by ancient Egypt. The discovery of Tutankhamun's tomb in 1922 had a great impact on fashion.

Square neckline

Heavy beading

The woman's partner wears full evening dress—a black tailcoat and pants, a black, or more usually white, waistcoat, and a white bow tie. For less formal evenings, a dinner jacket (without tails) could be worn, in which case the bow tie had to be black. These rules are still followed today.

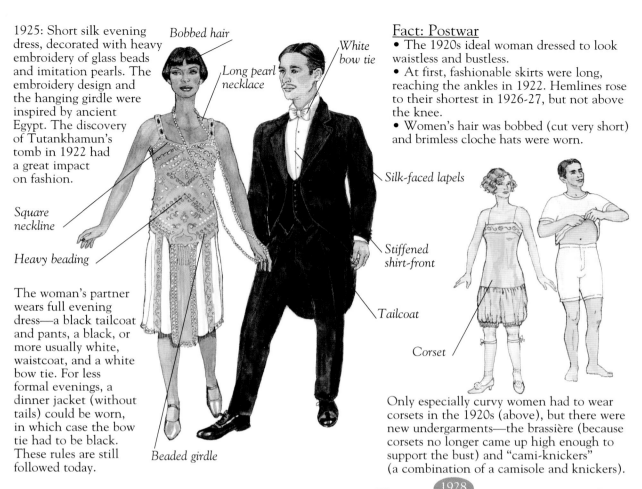

Bobbed hair

Long pearl necklace

White bow tie

Silk-faced lapels

Stiffened shirt-front

Tailcoat

Beaded girdle

Fact: Postwar

• The 1920s ideal woman dressed to look waistless and bustless.
• At first, fashionable skirts were long, reaching the ankles in 1922. Hemlines rose to their shortest in 1926-27, but not above the knee.
• Women's hair was bobbed (cut very short) and brimless cloche hats were worn.

Corset

Only especially curvy women had to wear corsets in the 1920s (above), but there were new undergarments—the brassière (because corsets no longer came up high enough to support the bust) and "cami-knickers" (a combination of a camisole and knickers).

1921: A "coat dress"—a front-buttoning garment designed to look like a two-piece, with a fox-fur stole.

1922: Men in smart town clothes with bowler hats. The woman wears a long day dress and the girl has a cloche hat.

1925: A low back is popular for evening. The hair is boyish but the gauzy floating panels are feminine.

1926: The shortest skirts yet.
1928: Cutting fabric on the bias makes clothes cling to the body.

1929: Longer daytime skirts—a day dress of spotted silk and a two-piece trimmed with monkey fur.

1930–1959

B y the thirties, ordinary people were becoming much more fashion-conscious. Despite widespread unemployment, those who worked had more spending power than in the past. Popular magazines, advertising, and the cinema were all great fashion influences. The new "casual" clothes appeared: shorts, slacks, and backless tops, as more people took up weekend activities and sunbathing became the new health craze. During the Second World War, all goods were in short supply and clothes had to be skimpy. "Make do and mend" was the slogan. No wonder that the 1947 "New Look", which required huge amounts of cloth for long, full skirts, was a fashion sensation.

1930s underwear (above): Lightweight elasticated corset, Y-front pants invented in 1934.

Fact: The Thirties
• The thirties look was long and slender, with calf-length skirts.
• Pants for women were now acceptable as sportswear, or for informal evenings when they were wide and looked like skirts.

Drooping skirts, drooping sleeves, long gloves, and little tilted hats created the mid-thirties "lady-like" look.

Permed hair

Hat with veil

Gathered sleeves

Gloves, still essential

Court shoes

Fur stole

1931: Beach pajamas for summer relaxation.

1933: Younger women liked sportswear with a masculine cut.

1933: Couple in evening dress. A dinner jacket is now acceptable for all but the most formal evening events.

1936: Double-breasted traveling coats. All the families wear hats and the children have leggings for warmth.

1943: A draped dress, square-cut jacket, and coat, all with boxy shoulders created with large shoulder pads.

1940s woolen suit

Hair cream in hair

Fair Isle pullover

Boxer shorts

Sock suspenders

Trilby hat

1947: "New Look" dress in plain black, which focuses attention on the new silhouette. A huge bow emphasizes the scooped neck.

Off-the-shoulder collar

Nipped-in waist

Long gloves

Ankle-strap shoes

In 1947, French designer Christian Dior showed a collection of clothes that became immediately famous as "The New Look". After the shortages of the Second World War, women were thrilled by his lavish use of material and totally new shape—rounded shoulders, tiny waists, and long, full skirts.

Stiff petticoats were needed under the fullskirts of the 50s. Also, a strapless bra for evening wear.

Ballerina-length full skirt

Matching jacket and pants (known as a lounge suit, left) was now the usual daytime wear. Checked tweed and knitted pullover (in place of a waistcoat) gives this outfit an informal air.

Fact: Forties and Fifties
• The 40s began with shorter skirts, padded shoulders, and square toes. They ended with swaying, full skirts, or very narrow ones with a kick-pleat to make walking possible.
• 50s styles were tight-waisted and big-busted until the 1958 waistless sack dress appeared.

1946 1947 1948 1948 1953 1955 1959 1954

1946: "Swagger" coat falling straight from the shoulders.
1947: "New Look" suit with swinging skirt.

1948: Dior suit with long narrow skirt, "fly-away" cuffs, and jacket stiffened to stand out at the hips.

1948: Couple in formal evening wear.
1953: Figure-hugging suit emphasizes rounded hips.

1954: Full-skirted summer dress in flowered cotton.
1955: A-line skirt and jacket, widening toward the hem.

1959: Pixie hats and rompers for children, shorter hemlines for adults. Even men's overcoats are shorter.

1960s–1990s

Raised hairstyle

Heavy eye makeup

Tight armholes

Above-knee hemline

Young people were earning more than ever in the 60s, and they had more money available to spend on fashion. Even after the Second World War, fashion meant clothes for women who wanted to look 25. Since teenagers became such important buyers of fashion in the 60s, designers and manufacturers looked to the youthful worlds of sports, pop music, and street fashion for inspiration. Pants, T-shirts, and sneakers became part of everyone's wardrobe. It was not the design, but the designer label, that made a difference.

1965: Silk minidress by French designer Yves Saint Laurent (left). Its "window pane" design was inspired by modern abstract painting. The dress was a success and was immediately copied by manufacturers who mass-produced cheaply for high-end shops.

High-buttoning jacket with wide lapels

Beatles hairstyle

• In the 60s, the majority of women wore miniskirts. Like the 1850s crinoline, it was a skirt style that was accepted by everybody.
• However, the miniskirt went out of favor quickly. In the winter of 1967–68 hems were suddenly at the ankles.

1968: Double-breasted suit of striped corduroy, by English designer Mr. Fish. Dazzling psychedelic colors were popular.

Bright boots

From the 60s onwards, cheap copies of designer clothes quickly made their way to high-street stores.

1961: Armpit-hugging "Jackie Kennedy" suit.
1962: Pant-suit—drainpipe pants and matching top.

1965: Street fashion—a "Mod" in hat, hipster pants, and turtleneck.
1966: Velvet pant suit for evenings.

1967: The 60s miniskirt at its shortest. Boots, the essential footwear, go thigh-high to meet it.

1970: Hippies reject commercial styles for peasant clothes, beads, caftans, and Afghan leather coats.

1972: For a short while, "hot pants" replace skirts, even for work.
1975: Romantic cotton maxi dress.

70s hippy-inspired dress by Bill Gibb; suit with wide lapels, patch pockets, and flared pants.

80s "yuppies" dressed to look like city bankers.

90s T-shirt and see-through skirt. The man's dark suit, shirt, and tie are appropriate for work or formal occasions.

Turban hat

Kipper tie

Shoulder pads

Small collar

Narrow tie

Tank top

Flared pants

Flaring ankle-length skirt

Platform shoes

Turn-ups

Thin jersey fabric

Office suit

Slimline pants

1977

1983

1984

1986

1993

1995

1998

1994

1977: Punk street fashion: "Mohican" hair, metal-studded, black leather jackets, fishnet tights.

1983: Power dressing for business women—maxi-coat, pant suit, shirt, and tie.

1984: Family in waterproof casuals.
1986: Simple clothes, fancy price, by Italian designer Giorgio Armani.

1993: Baseball hat, T-shirt, and jogging bottoms or jeans. Man in the "linen look"—designer suit, no tie.

1994: Sheath dress.
1995: Strappy shift dress.
1998: Combat pants (for both sexes) and bare midriff.

2000–2009

The millennium began with a new futuristic direction for fashion that came to be known as "Y2K fashion"—full of modern details and metallic fabrics. This didn't last long, and though technology and science continued to revolutionize—with the first iPod in 2001 and the mass adoption of smart phones—fashion became nostalgic. Vintage fashions from previous eras, in particular the 40s, 50s, 60s, and 80s, came back in favor. Alongside the nostalgia for the past came an awareness for the future and the importance of preserving the planet. This was reflected in the emergence of sustainable and Fair Trade fashion. These brands often adopted a global or ethnic style known as "boho", which became very popular with young women.

Hair slicked back in quiff

Metallic jacket

Black patent pencil skirt

Buckle detail at waist

2000s underwear: Shapewear pants for women became popular in 2000. These are foundation garments intended to give the wearer a slim and shapely appearance.

The popular style for male underwear was designer boxer shorts. These were often worn with low-rise jeans so that the designer label at the top was visible.

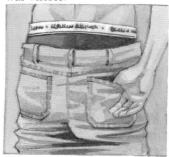

2000: Y2K style was often associated with people's infatuation with technology at the time.

2003: Designer print baseball hat, rugby shirt, and track pants (left). Bandana and low-rise jeans (right).

2004: Father and son in tailored tweed clothing. The flat cap became popular again.

2005: (left) Skinny jeans, soft sheepskin boots, oversized designer handbag, and sunglasses.

(right) 1980s revival: tartan print top, acid-wash jeans, and bright neon shoes.

2007: Military-style jacket with gold detailing and ornate trim.

2009: "Heritage"—tweed trench coat, bowler hat, and satchel purse—a quaint English look.

2004: "Boho chic" took inspiration from various bohemian and hippy influences.

2003: Vintage look: new or second-hand garments originating from a previous era.

Floppy hat

Major designers begin to take an interest in sustainable, Fair Trade clothing

Large faux-coin belt

Loose wavy hairstyle

Vintage 40s Victory roll hairstyle

Winged eyeliner and red lipstick

This particular look brought back a very feminine approach to high-end clothing with a strong emphasis on a woman's shape.

Tight 50s-style pencil-skirt dress with dogtooth pattern detailing

Big bangles

Black belt cinches waist

Fact: 2000 to 2009
• When the original iPod was introduced at the beginning of the 2000s, the gadget itself and even the earphones became somewhat of a fashion accessory.
• In 2005, skinny jeans were introduced. By spring 2006, sales had increased by 80 percent, making the skinny jean mainstream.

Black quilted clutch bag

Soft sheepskin boots

Floaty skirt made from light material

Youth fashion was strongly influenced by music-based subcultures, in particular emo, goth, and indie.

Dyed black hair

Black eye makeup

Neck scarf

Long hair and beard

Leather biker jacket

Long hair

Heavy eye makeup

Wristband

Denim shirt

All-black clothing

Skinny jeans

iPod

Checkerboard-pattern sneakers

Worn denim jeans

Fishnet tights

Heavy black buckled boots

Cowboy boots

Emo

Indie

Goth

2010–2014

Trends from the previous decade, such as vintage, were still fairly popular at first. However, 2010 saw a nostalgia for specific music scenes of the past, with 90s grunge becoming a major trend. Casual clothing was popular as well, as fashion took a far more relaxed approach than ever seen before with the adult "onesie". Colors could be minimalistic, even monochrome, or bold and bright with color blocking, which could be seen on many fashion runways.

2013: 1990s grunge made a comeback with distressed clothing worn in layers.

Beanie hat

2011: Color blocking— the combination of two or more bold colors— was popular.

Orange blazer

Oversized flannel shirt

Bright blue pants

Creeper shoes

- In 2014, a popular hairstyle for men was long on top and short on the sides.
- Beards and sleeve tattoos also came into the mainstream of fashion culture.

Sleeve tattoo

Beard

Fact: 2010 to 2014
- Colors such as teal, cobalt blue, pink, and neon yellow were extremely popular. These colors would often be combined in a color-blocking style (above right).

- The hair trend for women in 2012 was "ombre". This is when the ends of the hair are several shades lighter than the roots.

2011: (far left) "Geek chic": Man wears thick-rimmed glasses, bow-tie, suspenders, and sneakers. Woman wears Peter Pan collar, pleated skirt, thick-rimmed glasses, and brogues. (right) Maxi dress with sandals and jean waistcoat.

2012: Monochrome— black and white striped top, black tailored pants, and platform shoes.

2013: (left) Adult purple onesie and child animal onesie. (right) Man in green waxed jacket with turned-up jeans.

2014: Oscar de la Renta teal cashgora coat, Gucci black leather turtleneck, Michael Kors patent leather gloves. A futuristic look.

Glossary

bandana
A large brightly coloured handkerchief or neckerchief, which can be worn around your head or neck.

bias cut
A way of cutting fabric so that the threads of its weave will hang diagonally when worn. Normally they hang vertically and horizontally.

boater
A flat-crowned, stiff-brimmed straw hat, originally worn for boating.

bowler hat
A hard hat with a domed crown and a narrow curled brim.

brogue
Leather shoe with decorative perforations on the outer layer.

Burgundy
A rich independent state in the Middle Ages. Now part of eastern central France.

cameo
A precious stone or shell with two coloured layers. The top layer is partly cut away to create a design contrasting with the colour beneath.

camisole
A woman's undergarment.

cashmere
Costly Indian fabric made from the wool of the cashmere goats of the western Himalayas.

choker
A high neckline or necklace.

cocked hat
Hat with the brim folded against the crown in three places, giving it a triangular shape.

coif
Medieval close-fitting cap tied under the chin, worn by men and women, often under other headgear.

cravat
A piece of lace, linen or silk tied around the neck.

doublet
A man's short, front-opening overgarment, sometimes padded. It was worn from the 14th to the 17th centuries.

drawers
Undergarment for the lower part of the body and the upper legs. Originally it was formed of two pieces drawn up over each leg.

enamelled
An object decorated with melted glass of various colours.

flat cap
Rounded cap with a small stiff brim in front.

Franks
A Germanic people whose power extended over much of Germany and France from the 5th to the 9th centuries.

hippies
Followers of a 1960s lifestyle which rejected material values in favour of a loving, sharing and relaxed attitude.

hot pants
Very short shorts, briefly in fashion in the 1970s as a substitute for skirts.

kerchief
A piece of cloth covering the head.

kipper tie
A very wide tie worn in the 1970s.

loincloth
Male garment formed by tying a piece of cloth around the hips.

Mesopotamia
A region of the ancient world, roughly equivalent to modern Iraq.

muslin
Very fine, semi-transparent cotton fabric.

onesie
A loose-fitting casual jumpsuit for both children and adults.

raglan sleeve
Sleeve with a top extending to the neckline.

revers
The top part of the front opening of a jacket, folded back to show the lining .

slacks
Casual trousers usually of the pleated variety.

stomacher
A triangle of stiffened and decorated material placed between or over the front edges of a bodice.

trilby
Soft felt hat with a crease in the crown from front to back.

whalebone
A horny substance from the upper jaw of a whale. Used as a stiffener in women's corsets until the invention of plastic replaced it.

yuppies A 1980s term created from the initials Y, U and P (young, upwardly mobile persons). Used to describe pushy, newly successful people with plenty of disposable cash (money to spend).